To Joe,

My dear friend &

partner in crime!

Lots of Love

Patrick James :-)

2018.

IRELAND AGAIN
& OTHER NEW POETRY

IRELAND AGAIN
& OTHER NEW POETRY

Patrick James
www.patrickjames.ie

To order additional copies of this book, contact:
Xlibris Corporation
0-800-644-6988
www.xlibrispublishing.co.uk
Orders@Xlibris.co.uk
300404

CONTENTS

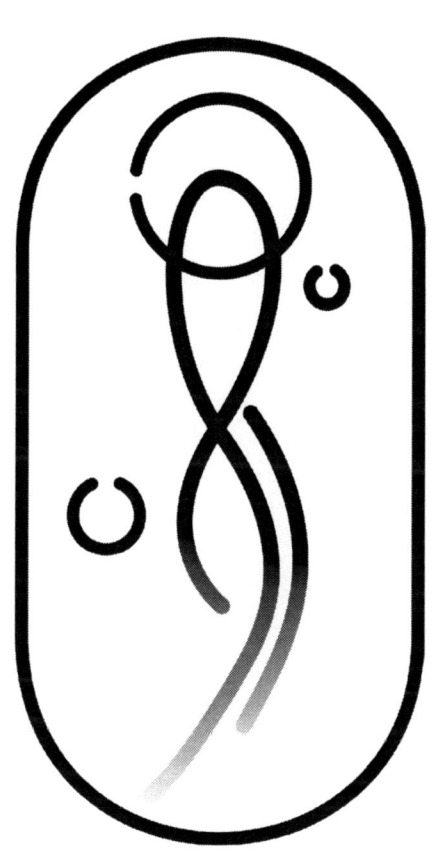

☯

When the sun's radiance
scorches the Earth's ground,
Nature sends her rains
as apologies to the flowers.

Written for my constant
"Inspiration" Maria
"My Friend, Lover and Friend".
The world is a brighter place simply
because you are in it.

To My Mum, Deirdre & Jack …
You are my poetry & I love you deeply.

Special thanks to
the gifted Jessica Baron Hughes
For the specially commissioned
cover painting "Ireland Again"

Ireland Again

Leaving behind the shorelines
of my beloved woman Ireland
in her hurt of lesser times,
I'd sailed for foreign sand.
Posting every coin earned
to those still back home,
reminds me of her character
and how I'm now alone.
I miss her ways and gurcake,
large families and ballads sung,
the trading along the quays
and the Liffey banks in flood.
An old man nearing life's end
I want to see Ireland again.

Reflections At W.B.'S Grave

"An old ghost's thoughts are lightning,
to follow is to die;".

Not wonder nor reverence;
an air of something else
enshrouds your rest place—
they look for splinters of
of your greatness to hold onto.
At an ever lifeless grave,
in face of your immortal
words they feign to console
themselves, for your station
is not among the dead.
Visitors remember you living
in The Wind Among The Trees
The Valley Of The Black Pig
and The Travail Of Passion.
Reading your memories' epitaph,
with wordless, empty expressions
they look as though they await
on you, for one last poem.

Regardless Of Shipbuilding

Walking home a little
past midnight,
it had hardly stopped
raining and cleared
the dockland air.
The moon, piercing the
sky was clearer still
like it could burst
and fall in snow-drifts;
as if it could almost
revive the lost fairy-tale
deep inside my spirit.

Your Emigrant Son

Your ghost was strong in me
tonight, fair Annalivia.
Softly singing of Dublin Streets
to an emigrant son,
like a busker on the breeze.
Whispering to me as I stroll
in a distant land New York;
gathering up my childhood memories
like a pickaroonie who hoards
collected cinders.
I think of mother's Gurcake,
and remember the homely
scent of Bewley's;
the kisses stolen at Ha'penny
Bridge and the walk
along the Liffey.
Remember me, fair Annalivia
for you're always strong in me,
like my memories as a Dubliner,
now an emigrant son.

Smoking Causes Cancers . . .

Smoking causes cancer—
and no-one seems
    to care,
as if cigarettes were trees . . .
   a book
is made of wood like
the match . . . *It*
     consumes
itself and dares to steal
a life—
  the flame quenched,
  its memory
lingers
  on as smoke,
    the Word
we write just turns to
    ashes.

That Voice Again . . . .

And as a child when
shadows came I followed
certain beliefs in a sword—
having heard the stories,
prayed to the *Holy Grail*
every morning for a
King's honour or the
promise of finding *Avalon* . . .
but what living demands
has reduced my dreams
to archaeology and doubts
in the origin of fairytales.

The Midsummer's Visitant

The midsummer's summer sun
girdles blue in golden apparition
as phantom Indian spirits hunt
in air's prairie of cloudy calm.
As heaven's purview burns
where fiery skyline visits earth,
as dusk adopts an ultraviolet hue
in middle-summer's berth.
The souls of a thousand years
have gathering gathered here;
the dead lovers and their dreams
alive again rise up in the heat
into the still dry air to chant
of lovers' wanton rapture,
on summer's midsummer night.

An Seol Briste

I'm like a sail that's seen
too much the sea,
too much the setting sun
having still not sailed enough.
Once handsome a time ago
racing gulls just off of shore,
racing waves to the horizon
my breeze has come and gone . . . .

Car Parking

My partner recently told
her friends that she really
did wish that I would take
the bus to work or walk . . .
the walls of Trinity college
are black with fumes off
the countless exhausts—
Molly Malone bears that
uncomfortable frown of
a woman suffering with
asthma and the Anna-Livia
has contracted lung-cancer
from her passive smoking . . .
and the great iron-railings
of Dublin weep for her.

Off The Coast of Cork

Last night and this sleeping
and dreaming . . . and I dreamt
that I could hear the voice
of two souls awaiting a third—
at first was limp and peaceful
like a drowning, then the second
voice, distraught, sounded alike
a person lost at sea awaiting
a rescue-boat.
Sleep was so unsettling then
and I woke up startled and
to a passing bewilderment, not
having heard their third soul—
the speaker who showed themselves
two days later as a headline . . .
that was the year a torpedo
sank the mailship Leinster.

Markings of a Past

Drafting a tribal
symbol onto my face
with Indian ink—
invisible to our senses,
the sensations on the
skin are indelible,
like memories of a
ghost's aura drawn
to a certain silence.

Four Times of *Her* . . . .

Imbolc—my whispers
come to life and
awake thoughts of
nursing snowdrops . . .

they stretch their petals
in my belly and
blossom as ideas.

Beltane—the awakening
world of *her* slowly
stimulates my body . . .

Lughnasa—I wear
the gold and oranges
and whites of marrying
her, having been
conceived in her womb—

Samhain—comes and
with it, I take comfort
in the calm white skin
of her soft bosom.

Handmades in Red

Colour setting into a
waxy skin—
carmine atoms settling
and slowly sinking
in the cooling blood,
like fallout dust
limited to the confines
of the candle-maker's
mould . . . once peeled
away forgets the past
and endeavours the
irony of reducing itself
into darkness, to carry
a flame for a single
night . . . .

The Empty Timberness . . . .

. . . and all the wood the
world throws up couldn't
build a bridge—

and there's a ravine
of silhouettes where
no trees grow and tools

of carpentry lie rusting
where wood-work remains
an abandoned art

and your last engraving
mentioned dreams of children

. . . and all the wood the
world throws up couldn't
build a bridge—

Gravitation

Sometimes, the reflection of the sun
can be so misleading—
a coin-size glimpse of day
in the middle-dark of night.
At other times a dolphin, swimming
unseen without a sound or love,
in a deepest blue called midnight.

The Aching of Light . . . .

From the womb of hives—
enjoying candle-making
in the evenings
after work . . . al*one,*
and occasionally wonder

if a certain bee lost
their life to defend
what *their* gathering made . . .
these white, melting
pearls of wax or

reluctantly fall lethargic
in bee-keeper's smoke—
having worked a setting
rouge into columns
of marble and performed

caesarean on their moulds,
I christen their birth
on a table set for two,
as I unwittingly learn
about the stings a woman's
pregnant body lovingly carries . . . .

The Old Players

All but too well—
a little worried is
Autumn for Winter—
the revolting re-birth
of *that* tragic-hero
come February . . . .

Ma mere, the Alligator

'*Ma mere*' has always
been an alligator—
she remembers the great
age of her species, their
swimming with soft cadenced
strokes and her ancestors
in the Amazon (def: *n.* female
warrior of legend; tall, strong
woman).

She would make a sound
like hissing or a fearsome
roar during mating season
or in warding off unwelcome
intruders—after her mating
she had constructed a nest,
inearthing her child egglings
in the warm damp sands
and the comfort of mud
until we had hatched in
the heat of the sun.

Our father was killed by
a hunter's rifle for *his*
leather but my mother still
stood guard in the heat—
then without hurting us, she
carried her infants in her
mouth to the water's edge.

Overlooking the Ocean

I saw my own image
floating on its own
reflection—
and all that changed
it, however, slightly,
were the calm ripples
of time fading out
on the shoreline . . .

Season of Snow

Suns giving up their skyline,
seasons ending, winter comes—
in these last days loved ones
leave too soon, still in our time,
our branches left to mourn
those loved migrating birds.

Deserted but for shivering robins
who linger on with memories
of warmer weather, a little hope
in spite of all death's vanity—
tiny red-breast seems stained
with passing away or grieving
watching worlds change places.

Life-filled autumn lakes, eyes,
which I'd seen struggling for
time before freezing over;
currents beneath smiling up
one last and eternal smile
as if reddish dusk in summer;
but this is melting snowfall
falling anew as shattering tears
for a beloved bird has flown.

In A Trice

My time is told on a plastic watch-
a play-thing easily broken or lost;
mindfully designed to appear realistic.
Thinking back, it's as although
the smaller second hand has been
the faster all along; too quick
to stop and count the many days
or weigh up each human thought.
Meanwhile, the greater copper time-piece
which the clock-maker made
to last, ticks on consistently.

The Green Goddess

We turn our back on Nature,
the Goddess of all creation—
build monstrous cities against
her skyline and new machines
to scratch away her soul.
We look up for other planets,
perhaps, as to no longer fear
this woman's godly hold—
our mere existence is a mockery
for she alone, speaks through us.
Regardless, in time or when
our imagination has granted
us means enough, she will be
the one whose love will let
us go—
to search for another Goddess,
knowing, immaterial of likeness
there'll never be another Earth.

Dolmen

(The Priestess Diane's Journey)

Strawberry-blonde of forgotten Celtic-fire,
pagan rituals of love re-enkindled
from ashes scattered across our world,
awakens in one woman's earthly desires.
A druidic wind whispering of woodland
spirits, breezes through the empty winter
streets of sleepy Massachusetts, silhouetted
again a purple skyline's pastel contrast.
The spirit of bronze-age religion, a ghost
spiralling across the many ages, returning
once again as what is meant to be,
encircles one woman, her witch's soul.
In an antiques shop in Salem, I heard
someone say that she was everything—
her deep brown eyes watching waterfalls,
her altar-offerings of candles and loose-earth.
An expressive-sensuous smile, stirs deities
of the sun with its enchanting warmth.
Entering our jade coloured land of kings
she'd journeyed the world's seas
having heard Nature softly calling, calling,
calling her, as our ancestors before.

Grafton-St.-fluidic

Watching our liquid sunshine
pouring down on passers-by
to morning work, anonymous

gusts of black and psychedelic
brushing off one another in
cursory zigzags above their
head-long faces—
an hour before was silence,
a *drunken-silence* in door-
ways . . . street lights closing

their eyes unnoticed as dawn
climbs over the roof-tops,
whispers down the twilight,
lifeless concrete and slowly into
the closed up shops and cafés . . . .

The Look of Division

Every night could bring
the sounds of *sirens'*. . .
calling to *him* in the
silent distance of *his*
safety—someone would
always answer the fate
of *their* song with a
journey in an ambulance,
but these nights were
the place where *he*
grew-up and where
living found him, sometimes
wading in whiskey—
streets, which a love
stole his soul back from . . .
unable to set it free.

Moon Imagenesis

rain bringer
and Woman of
t*ide*s:
consort of every
mystery, whose
        name
cannot be spoken—
entering
darkness, naked.
We purify
and cast a circle,
engulf
our-self/ves in
energy and
inspiration,
i/mage/imagination:
sensitivity
        and initiation,
another closure
before
a new beginning.
        Our Moon,
hidden, uncovers
secrets
of the shoreline . . .

We are
open to our
    own
spirits and each
other,
    meditating
and chanting on
these three nights
    of Sisterhood—
having earthed
the Centre symbol
we feast with
  Her
and open the
Circle . . .

The Course

One morning beginning in July,
having left our various worlds
for a little while to learn
of another world's ways,
We set out on a journey
together as a crew of
curious new recruits—
everyone, a unique new
stranger, *they* each brought
a different skill aboard as
we cast-off onto unknown waves
to study the nature of sailing.
Following our *Captains'* maps
and careful compass headings
we became shipmates but in
the weaving of ropes and the
unravelling of sails on a maiden
voyage, we discovered friendship.

Cocooned

Your body is warm
around me and even
though I love you
I must leave—
It is your fortune to
gently release me . . .
I am a butterfly.

Prophecy of Celtic Ancient's Revisited

Clarions sound out aloud
in the Hibernian far-off hills
calm brass voices melodiously sound
of a reborn past's future will;
when tides turning around—
their crested pearls still
and steady wash back
onto the forgotten beach
of time's gone-by sands—
the reign of women's femininity.
Water-flow harmonies of harps
awaken ancient Celtic ideas;
Nature's blood of Breton culture
flows and fills up every vein,
as musical flutes return
our beliefs to the ways
of woman's empathy with Nature—
a religion again feminine based.
Acclaiming once more her wise-soul
and gentle creativity of birth;
her Nature-imbued feminine soul
and its constant gift to the Earth.

The Return to Lir

Poured from the arch of
the moon into the glass
of my awakening heart . . .
Love came easily as a
crazy thing of beautiful—
Perfect blue eyes mirroring
my own soul lead me on
towards entering a golden
ring, to bear children
and live out our lives
as tenderly mated Swans,
for this is the One.

Indelible

My mother could sew
a button on or stitch
up a seam—
I always had a hand
knit Aran woollie growing
up, to keep me warm
and even now . . . that
box of needles and
thread, which she kept
in the press, reminds me
of humankind—
sometimes it reminds me
of nothing at all but my
inability to sew . . . or the
perfume she wore when
she was going out.

Creeps

Beetles underneath tacked floor-
boards keep the secrets of
your room—they have heard

your groaning and looked at
you through gaps in the wood . . .
the sight of your naked female

form fails to intrigue them and
you take comfort in their calm
indifference towards your body—

you enjoy the irony that *men*
cannot fly on miniature black
wings nor walk on their bellies.

Dún Laoghaire

Wharf: *n* a platform at
    harbour, on river
    etc. for loading and
    unloading ships.

Since I've been here
I've heard so many
people note that *this*
was their most favoured
place . . . and seen so
many setting their sails
but everyone passes *here*
sooner or later—
they leave with stories,
set for foreign shores,
words which bring our
Viking-sailors home.

Bisection

(written at a loved-one's grave).

In your decrepit days of now
waiting and of worry and of
losing hope, where *when* becomes
vague present, I glimpsed your
ghost's reflection in my daughter's
first steps.

She loves her young life, the
everything of colours and sound
and shapes—her hands intrigue
her mouth with Lilliputian fists
and time itself seems derelict with
its own too breakable fullness.

Invocation

Transforming,
  always renewed—
your first visible
    crescent
appearing
slowly, the
pattern remaining
the same
always:
She creates
a sacred
space in darkness
    among
our rituals.
Earth,
the womb awakens
    from sleep:
inspiration, insight
        and healing—
tide turns
  and clarity
of vision, *She*
invokes
what *We*
visualize
growing;
    and we end
our ceremony by
opening
the Circle—
a waxing moon
  filling up we
await the realization
of change.

No Archangelic Supper

Culture

offered clay once in return
for crops or even land to plough,
scattered wheat seeds on

broken ground God had forgotten;
turned from then heathen deities
to worship one man's word.

Prayer

in passing became our question:
what sort of Father sets
a single place for a son

at his table then tells
his other children, he will
love them more when they are

dead.

Poem, Paint, The Creation[1]

I talked with the stars and the moon;
We discussed humility and its importance;
They told me I was the poem, not the poet;
I was not the painter but the paint,
nor the creator, I was the creation;
Stars whispering in my ears,
moon writing in my thoughts;
Climb the tree to the top,
you've no wings, why would you try
to fly?
Humility will help bring peace in your
soul;
Life holds many difficulties,
make not more by creating falsehoods out
of ego;
You'll only go up, then you'll fall;
I listened, for the stars were clever
and the moon was wise,
for I am the poem, the paint, the creation;

---

[1]   Originally published '93 under the pseudonym '*The Sandman.*'

Earthwomb

God is she . . .
and her likeness godly.

Divine and maternal woman
symbols Earth's godly form
her womb does eternity summon,
a lovely meaning it has borne.

A passage through a universe
for Earth alike womb grants birth.

Months in womb of Mother
analogous are to years in life;
nurtured before passing another
birth into another womb and time.

Born from Earthwomb through
water we find new youth.

Woman is not poetic mystery—
she is feminine and earthly,
she is gentle in the form
of our maternal Earth God.

Bedroom Hearts

Kisses mapped onto fleshes—
naked, ornate and intimate,
road-signs to your soul
drove us on towards now
and here after making out
we lie as motionless as cars
abandoned in the desert—
sweat lightly rusts our skin,
the lamp beside this bed
reflected on our stomachs
as a sun too hot to bear.
Tomorrow, you will see your
husband again and I know
that not even tenderness,
our tenderest of moments,
can kiss your bruising
better, each time he hits
you.

Ymir

(The Body Of The New World.)

The age of ice and snow
and snow-lands to the north
being warmed by the sun-land's
fervent breath began to melt;
hence, Ymir the primeval frost giant
was born of a thawing planet.
Suckling on the milk of Audhumbla—
Mother-Earth, he took his dynastic seat
among the Titans before being murdered
brutishly and his dominion succeeded
by the deific architects of the world.

In the dynast Ymir's deicide,
his dead body was hewed into the
new world, between the estate of fire
and the snow's glacial realm.
His flesh became the land, his blood,
the sea and his bones the mountains.
The welkin's abode was the skull
wherein the thoughts were clouds.

The globe had been founded
as it should best remain,
yet Ymir has soon grown elderly;
the body which now lies fragile
is being drained of its vitality.
The snow-lands are vanishing away
and the noble blood is poisoned;
our ancestor's thoughts weigh heavy,
confounded by the whim to destroy
what is fundamental to our survival.

Love Poem

Woe not come eventide
or its slow sleepy sunset—
nor in the night it summons,
for with more than eyes
I'll gently greet your duskiness—
same as I welcome your light.

Blush

I watched a kind of clouds
gathering on her sallow cheeks
as a kind of evening skyline,

in which certain herdsmen find
their assurances of better days—
and I wonder what intimate

thought, passing like a person
built out of dwindling snowfall
had hidden beneath that face:

moments behind old photographs,
unseen or simply kept secret . . . .
a kind of fraying line seeping

between pornography and privacy,
and maybe the skin of beauty
is a trivial thing, that suffers

a kind of Narcissus curse found
only in the fading of innocence;
found only in that first blush . . . .

Mid-morning Smog

Brittle . . . like smoke smothering
a match to suffer its own
likeness . . . that secret hurting
deep inside and that sometimes
feeling, that if not for skin
imprisoning the pain we could
weep our souls into the fibres
of our solar-system unnoticed—
maybe stumble into nothingness
quite willing but for bones . . .
to become the cry of a wolf
and imagine the loneliness of
the wilderness . . . just like life
in the suburbs.

Ascension

"what is sown a natural body
rises up a spiritual body" (1 Cor. 15:44).

Lying me out in a manner
similar to the crucifixion,
the restoration in sacred blood

and the marvel of what would
follow—A dove's first heart-beat
whispering in a mother's stomach,

conceived of our human bodies.
Accompanying my wife to share
in hearing the ultrasound—

Imagining my infant child's first
endeavours with words, straining
for syllables, consonants gradually

discovering vowels, their saying
mama later becoming dada.
Next, our hopes became tragedies

of unanswered prayers, all at
once and before a first breath
was taken a dove had been

drowned in blood, my love's
swollen bosom, betrayed by
milk our baby will never suckle.

Her Beautiful Reward

Heavy rain having been and
fallen hard had cleared the air—
the muddy ground looked fertile
in her August mating ritual.
Rains she sent up were the hand
she caressed herself with—
her frustration after the heat,
the build up of a long summer.
Touching herself, she begins lightly
building up into a downpour—
finished, her whole body still,
her skies are blue and bright.

The Pirate Lascar

Faithful true and endearing
my love's requite is furnished
by my lover's lovely ear—
her devotions of inert listening.
As light journeys the universe
to fall on a planet's love,
to lie again' my lover's breast
I've voyaged a moonlit world.

Like perfume shed by nymphs
onto night-time's silver waters
of a handsome pirate's ocean,
my reckless ardour imperils all
of my smuggler crew
as I go ashore sea's most wanted.
her damp lips' soft bouche
reforms my wild uncivil tenet,
and hence my visiting by dark.

As day dawns on the harbour
the admiral's tender daughter
bids me take my leave, for
dangers lurk most everywhere.
and with the words "*you handsome
sailor,*" she drops one tear,
for despite our deathless rapture
we may never once walk together
in the sea-breeze of morning.

Stealing myself away from the
anchorage of her feminine embrace,
I leave her company with the scent
of her body's fragancy on my raiments.
appearing on the brumous beach
I have befallen at my ambush—
a naval host of muskets fifty
and a cannoneer to attend my capture.

Nonetheless for brave struggle
I fell captive to a shot wound
and taken to a damp dungeon,
to await an executioner's noose.
Lying abated on a wet stone,
my only thoughts are of my lover
and the nights we have known,
as I write my last billet ever

to tell her of my love,
before acceding to my charge.

Lilies or Reeds[2]

You always were warm in me
my river of dreams.
Are you flowing tightly around
my leaves, could "Love You"
lie?
Now the oceans that feed have
caused you hurt, made you
choose;
Questioned you with him or me,
lilies or the reeds.
Will you flow to him to quench
his needs;
Will you be to me the waters
I drink, will I be the one you
clean?
If this one is real, for me a
single orchid as you my river
bathe me.

---

[2]   Originally published '92 under the pseudonym '*The Sandman.*'

Children

Nature's maternal energy
having been pleased
by love's warm ritual,
sends those little spirits
of her innocence—
harmless orbs of light
which softly guide
all lovers back to her.

In the Shadows

As I hurry by shadows in the
vampire hour, I cloak my face
for I'm the forgotten, but for
my lover's heart.
The villagers saw of me wrong
and cursed our love as evil,
all 'cause I lived an estranged
living, yet you, loved me even
in my gentle silence—
now, having been forbidden, we
quietly meet behind the shadow's
veil of night where I hide, and
secretly kissing as we'd walk in
the silhouettes, through the rainy
streets and court yard.
If ever I am caught they swear
I'll surely hang; they may chase
me via daylight for ever having
loved you, but as long as you
await me in the shadows, I'll
gently go stalking their nights.

Homecoming

My memories are alike captains
as I take the run-down ferry
to her town beside the ocean—

there was once a booming fishing
industry but that's all changed
now, still, San Sebastian keeps

its promises for me in a name.
We were young when we met one
another and the years have passed

by untouched or even sleeping
waiting to be awoken with a kiss—
the wedding-like-photo, much worn

has done its duty to my love . . .
it has resisted lonely impatience
in a foreign country and brought

> me home.

Metallurgic

Metallic voices . . .
    heartbeats
once the lights
have been turned out.
Mind, mouth . . .
and feelings swelling,
to feel skin uncovering
  our softer natures—
the things
we bury
in warm soils of
sacred grounds . . .
Fingers working
    their way
back to the tenderness
of holding—
  falling
asleep together
having made metal
    sing—
sweet metallic voices
seeping into
the daring
  concrete of your
      bones . . . .

Hate From Heat

When we are one another
we'll really hate ourselves—
the secrets I knew you hid
would have all been said;
the ghosts you once cremated,
returning to possess me within.
Fantasies you locked away
behind smiles you said were
for me, as Medusa's stare
would show their face to mine.
Our most painful I love you
becoming her sweetest fuck you;
to know what we once had—
the teenage dreams of liking,
the heat and fucking lies.

A Summer's Rose

A damp soft room where angels
sing beautiful harmony, perhaps
of the perverted kind but this
was destiny leaving us blush
and love, and love.

Damn, beautifully beautiful how
the waves of her golden hair
rolled down her back, gentle as
moon beams whispering to the
secrets of lovers in summer.

Touching sensually touching, she
blossomed like a red, red rose,
sensual rain drops soaking the
scented petals softly caressed by
kissing and beautiful feelings,
pouring across my lips like rays
of sun.

Beneath this gentle summer's
moonlight we fill our embrace
with eroticism as we blush and
breath deeper and love, and
breath deeper as nature takes us
tenderly in arms turning our bodies
into one, as we dance this dance
as summer lovers.

Our bodies flowing into one unity
of nature like a red, red rose
growing beautifully aside a mountain
spring, as angels sing their beautiful
sensual song, leaving us blush and
love, and love.

My Autumn Down-pour

Now, the rain has a voice
i recognize and whispers to
the world, as it sleeps, of
what the heart just beneath
the silence is feeling—
the world, seems to be, being
washed away by this Autumn
storm and the only emotion
able to swim appears to be
my loneliest longing for home . . . .

Our mourning in *Spring*

These are days when the
rains come, entering the
soul . . . and yet, feelings
of tears seem distant
as the *Earth* gives thanks
with the things of rebirth,
which visit our home
with *Her* onset of April . . .

Primate

Should I need to climb trees,
I wouldn't ask a fish to teach me—
I'd seek the guidance of a monkey.
If ever I wanted to learn to fly
I'd never consult an ostrich
though for all appearances it is
a bird, I'd rather ask an eagle.
Similarly, if I wanted to find
religion, I'd never ask a priest.

Tomorrow's child . . .

Looking out towards a
doorway at *Newgrange*
at the dawn Millennium—
the *Middle-world* of our
spirits, as *We* are slowly
reborn in a pagan Sunrise
to *our* beautiful Country
of the unknown promise,
kept secret by infant *Time* . . . .

Lover's Leap

I'll wait for you in
the heroin shadows
of my bloodshot mind
before we take a boat
out into that darkness
of infinite space—
into one another's hand-
cuffed arms . . .

Conceived at Newgrange

Every night I visit
your empty cradle—

a bewildered *Sandman*
wondering just where
your history begins . . .

with Beltane or Lughnasa
and are you like a
belly dancer completing
another circle of her
womb and if winter
has been barren so
far, can I still keep
faith in *her* promise
of spring or bearing-fruit . . . .

Charcoal

Lowered into wet darkness
during our Civil-war,
the earth, soon dried off

your bones—the faded
paint in the chiselled-out
grooves of some epitaph

and collapsing wreaths . . .
apparently abandoned twenty
years ago, a now remote

reminder that our old war-
heroes had once been loved.
Now, no-one visits your

grave bar the odd stray
animal which occasionally
relieves themselves on the
   battalion of nettles.

Excavation

It could have
been a cemetery
Eden—
once,
we played among
its orchards
then
the grave-robbing
begun.
Unearthing
a pile of bones,
they soon put
them back together
in the
shape of a woman—
tied up at her
wrists and ankles
the rope cut
into their marrow.
The blood soaked
cords loosening
turned to
serpents—
winding around
the Eve and
slowly turning
her on she
conceived a
child and named
him Adam . . .
and then there
was the grave-robbing.

Anchor

Overboard and floating
down, bubbles sauntering
upwards from my lungs
as they fill up with water . . .
becoming enthralled by the
mysteries of the deep—
an octopus, its magnificent
shades changing colours,
swims up to inspect my
corpse . . . intrigued by
this blueish, lifeless thing . . . .

Beautiful Rebuilding

Hearing a whisper like
Winter, a look like ashes
and smelt of a heavy
morning fog on suburbia—

once, tried to live deep
inside, unable to hear
sounds the heart requests—

and building a cabin
out of wood I saw the
Earth again, imagined that
Carpenter's expression as
He held *His* infant child.

The Vision Chimes

These exploring fingers
of *Her*, when Moon
makes space in the
day for certain prayers—
or during each month
for worship—these
invisible caresses of
sensation pushed
into *her Lunar* belly—
this uncontrived intimacy
which turns the tides,
from sleep to swelling . . . .

Email to Heaven

(for my dear dad)

Time has slowly made me
older and more like my father.
When my poems are like prayers
and the letters I send from
my computer, seem to head out
into an abyss half finished,
I am left awaiting a reply
and quite simply remembering—

I was a child again and my
father was there again and
I could understand how his
gentle ways would guide my
life into adulthood later on.
In the chair next to his my
mother was smiling and laughing
at the two men in her life . . .
and that is why my prayers
for a reply are so much
more for her, than for me.

And another night passes by
when I wipe a little tear
from the corner of my eye.
as I prepare to go out into
the world to finish my letters . . .
and I am left wondering,
if my emails can make it
through to heaven to my father.

Lightning Source UK Ltd.
Milton Keynes UK
04 December 2010

163813UK00002B/16/P